My Science Notebook
Inventions
By Martine Podesto

Please visit our web site at **www.garethstevens.com**.
For a free catalog describing Gareth Stevens Publishing's list of high-quality books,
call 1-800-542-2595 (USA) or 1-800-387-3178 (Canada).
Gareth Stevens Publishing's fax: 1-877-542-2596

Library of Congress Cataloging-in-Publication Data
Podesto, Martine.
    Inventions/by Martine Podesto.
        p. cm.—(My Science Notebook)
    Includes bibliographical references and index.
    ISBN-10: 0-8368-9214-3 (lib. bdg.)
    ISBN-13: 978-0-8368-9214-7 (lib. bdg.)
    1. Inventions—Juvenile literature. I. Title.
    T48.P62   2008
    600—dc22   2008012429

This North American edition first published in 2009 by
Gareth Stevens Publishing
A Weekly Reader® Company
1 Reader's Digest Rd.
Pleasantville, NY 10570-7000 USA

Gareth Stevens Senior Managing Editor: Lisa M. Herrington
Gareth Stevens Creative Director: Lisa Donovan
Gareth Stevens Senior Designer: Keith Plechaty
Gareth Stevens Associate Editor: Amanda Hudson
Special thanks to Joann Jovinelly

Photo Credits:
p. 26: Shutterstock; p. 50: Vic Aboudara/iStockPhoto.com; p. 62: Shutterstock; p. 71: Hélène Brion;
p. 81: Craig Hammel/Corbis

Every effort has been made to trace the copyright holders for the photos used in this book, and
the publisher apologizes in advance for any unintentional omissions. We would be pleased to
insert the appropriate acknowledgments in any subsequent edition of this publication.

My Science Notebook
Inventions

By Martine Podesto

Science and Curriculum Consultant:
Debra Voege, M.A., Science Curriculum Resource Teacher

Gareth Stevens
Publishing

Table of Contents

Dear Reader,

So many **inventions** have changed the way we live. Inventions make our lives better. Each invention has an amazing story. Many young readers think stories about inventions are interesting, too.
So, I've gathered questions about some of my favorite inventions.

Who invented the wheel? When was ice cream first created? How long has paper been around? I've answered these questions and many others in this notebook, with simple diagrams, photos, and other illustrations.

Keep asking questions and let your imagination run wild. Who knows? You may be one of tomorrow's great inventors.

Happy reading!
Professor Brainy

Dear Emily,

That's a very interesting question! As a matter of fact, fire is not really an invention. Let me explain the difference between an invention and a **discovery**.

An invention is something new that is created by a human being. It is something that did not exist before. It can be an object, a tool, or a material. A discovery is something that already existed in nature, but was understood for the first time. And so, Emily, fire is a discovery and not an invention.

Keep in mind, however, that all the different ways to make a fire are inventions. (Think of a lighter or matches, for example.)

But let's get back to your question. One of the oldest clues that humans used fire was found in a cave in South Africa. Fossilized bones from millions of years ago showed that people at that time had cooked an antelope. It is believed that, when lightning struck bushes or trees and lit them on fire, prehistoric humans managed to carry a flame home. How did they do it? No one knows for sure. But it's possible that a brave member of the tribe approached this huge fire to light a stick of wood. The tribe would have probably watched over the flame, day and night. It was important that the fire stay lit. They did not yet know how to start it themselves!

It was a million years later that humans invented the first ways of making fire. This discovery changed people's lives. From this moment on, people could use fire to frighten off wild animals and to cook meat and vegetables. Also, thanks to the light from the flame, they could make homes in caves that had once been too dark to live in. We are used to using fire now, but at the time, it was a huge change!

Kind regards,
Professor Brainy

Dear Raymond,

As far as we know, the first object invented was a tool. The tool was a **chopper**—a stone carved with another stone to make it sharp. Its inventor was one of the first humans, called *Homo habilis*. The chopper was practical! It was used to cut up the meat of animals (perhaps antelopes or elephants), carve wood, or crack nutshells. The oldest of these carved stones were found in Tanzania, a country in East Africa. They are more than 2.5 million years old. Over time, improvements were made to this tool. After choppers, people

Chopper

made **bifaces**. These stone tools, often made of a rock called flint, were carved on two sides. The result was a narrow and very pointy tool as sharp as glass! Little by little, new tools were invented for specific tasks. People

Biface

carved stones in pointy shapes to make spears and arrows for hunting. They sharpened small bones to make sewing needles and fishhooks.

Huge progress was made, Raymond, thanks to these tools. They made it possible for people to make clothes, hunt, build houses, and...invent more tools!

Fondly,
Professor Brainy

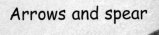
Arrows and spear

Dear Professor Brainy,
Can you tell me who invented writing?

Thanks a lot.
Anna, age 10

Dear Anna,

Writing is one of the greatest human inventions. Thanks to writing, we can record facts and information. It's hard to imagine life without writing, isn't it? It all started with the earliest humans, who quickly felt the need to share thoughts and information, and write about their daily lives.

The first words were written more than 5,000 years ago by the **Sumerians**. They lived on the banks of the Tigris and Euphrates rivers in what is now Iraq. Each word was represented by a different drawing. This early writing had about 2,000 signs! Over the centuries, it changed. The drawings that represented objects became simple nail-shaped strokes. We call this **cuneiform**, or "wedge-shaped" writing. I'll let you see for yourself the way that the word "bird" evolved.

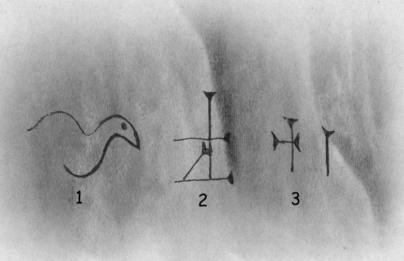

Little by little, each ancient civilization invented its own system of writing. Over time, the Greek, Chinese, and Egyptian writing systems were created.

Each form of writing changed on its own. New forms appeared, while others died out. This is why there are so many different kinds of writing today.

Take care,
Professor Brainy

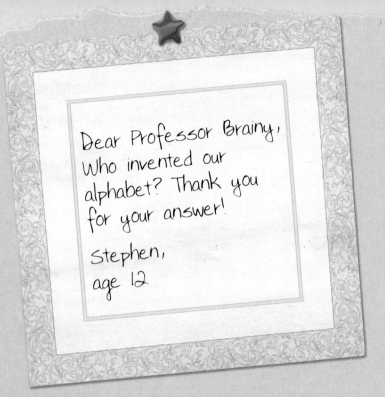

Dear Professor Brainy,
Who invented our
alphabet? Thank you
for your answer!

Stephen,
age 12

Dear Stephen,

"ABCDEFG... HIJKLMNOP... now I know my ABCs, next time won't you sing with me..."

To find out who invented this alphabet, also called the Latin alphabet, let's go back to Sumerian writing. With its 2,000 different little drawings, this writing was very difficult to learn and remember! Imagine that, to write correctly, you had to know all these signs. It wouldn't be easy! To solve this problem, the

Phoenicians (a people who lived on the east coast of the Mediterranean Sea) invented an alphabet made up of 22 consonants. Those consonants represented all the sounds in the Phoenician language. Their alphabet was the ancestor of our Latin alphabet. This was about 3,300 years ago. Five hundred years later, the Greeks perfected the invention by adding vowels to it. They also added early forms of punctuation. They called this series of letters the alphabet. The word is a combination of the first two letters in the Greek alphabet: "alpha" and "beta."

Four hundred years later, the Romans were inspired by the Greek alphabet to make their own system. They kept 19 of the Greek letters and invented 7 others. The Latin alphabet was born, with its 6 vowels and 20 consonants!

Best regards,
Professor Brainy

Dear Sophie,

Your question brings back wonderful memories. I remember the scent of the perfume my grandmother wore—and of my father's cologne when he picked me up to give me a hug. When I smell these scents, I remember them both.

To get back to your question, Sophie, no one really knows who invented perfume. We do know that it has been around a very long time. The Sumerians were using perfume about 5,000 years ago. It was the people of ancient Egypt, however, who perfected it.

The Egyptians considered perfume to be sacred. They burned **incense** to honor their gods. It was fashionable for them to rub perfumed grease on themselves.

Queen Cleopatra, who ruled Egypt more than 2,000 years ago, loved perfume. She had the fabrics around her soaked with it—even the sails on her boats! Legend has it that this was how she charmed the Roman emperor Julius Caesar. The Egyptians passed their love of perfume on to the Romans and the Greeks. The Romans were the first to capture these scents in glass bottles.

Perfume in ancient times was made from flowers, plants like rosemary, or scented wood like cinnamon. These scented plants were dipped into vegetable or animal oil, because oil traps scents. All one had to

Incense

do was burn the oil or rub it on oneself to release the scent.

Today, scented oils and plants are no longer needed for making perfume. Scientists recreate natural scents and invent new ones. How about you, Sophie? Do you have a favorite perfume?

Best wishes,
Professor Brainy

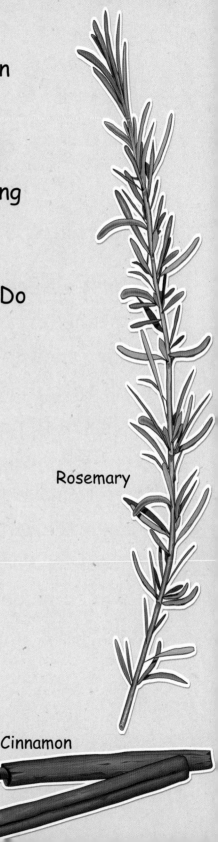

Rosemary

Cinnamon

Dear Gerald,

The first adventurers to explore the water were prehistoric humans. Ten thousand years ago, they took to the waves using tree trunks dug out with stone tools. Early on, people used their hands to paddle through the water. Later, they pushed long wooden poles along the bottom to move the boat. This worked better, but when the water was too deep, the poles were useless. Prehistoric sailors then invented oars, which helped steer boats in deep water.

Hollowed-out trunk

Egyptian sailboat

Boats have been changing ever since. People made boats for many purposes. They used them to fish, explore, and trade.

About 5,500 years ago, the ancient Egyptians began building sailboats. Powered by the wind, their boats were able to move heavy goods. For more than 6,000 years, people continued to build and improve upon sailboats.

The steamboat was invented in 1783. It had a large wheel with blades called paddles. A steam engine made the wheel turn. When the paddles pushed the water, they made the boat move. Wind was no longer needed. This was big progress!

Caravel
(15th century)

Boats today move faster than ever, thanks to propellers and huge diesel engines. They can cross the ocean in a very short time. Caravels, a type of boat used by 15th century explorers, took 70 days to sail from Spain to the Caribbean. The *Queen Mary II*, one of the newest ocean liners, does it in seven days. That's 10 times faster!

Your friend,
Professor Brainy

Wheel

Steamboat

Dear Professor Brainy,

When was money invented?

Take care,

Juan, age 11

Dear Juan,

That's a very interesting question! The first coins appeared in Lydia (now Turkey) about 2,650 years ago. What did people do before this invention? They **bartered**. This means they exchanged one service or object for another. Here is an example...

Suppose you went to an ice cream store. Without money, the only way to pay for your ice cream would be to make a trade: an ice cream cone for your mom's aprons. Of course, for this exchange to make sense, the objects

had to be of equal value.
In this case, the three
aprons would have been
valuable to an ice-cream man.
For example, he wouldn't get his
clothes dirty selling ice cream!

Long ago, people used valuable
goods like seashells, livestock, salt,
or metal to buy an object or service.
This method of exchange was not perfect.
Livestock were hard to handle and objects
like metal bars had to be weighed to find
their value.

Macedonian
coins

Gallic
coins

The first coins to appear in Lydia were made of electrum. Electrum is a natural mixture of gold and silver. The river that ran through the country was full of it. The coins had the symbol of the king on one side and a symbol on the other side that guaranteed the coin's value. This system was also adopted by Lydia's neighboring countries.

Lydian coins

And so, during the 400 years that followed, hundreds of cities began making their own money. From then on, money made exchanges easier.

Money has changed a lot since then. Today, you can pay for items with coins, bills, checks, or even credit cards.

Enjoy your ice cream!

Professor Brainy

Dear Professor Brainy,
My favorite sport is hockey. I would really like to play on a team, but not right away because I don't know how to stop yet! Can you tell me who invented ice skates?

Martin, age 10

Hello, Martin,

That's funny! I asked my father the same question when I was your age. The question popped into my head when he took me to watch a hockey game. You will probably be as surprised as I was by his answer. Ice skates have been around for more than 3,000 years! They come from Scandinavia, a region in northern Europe.

The skate blades were made from the bones of a large animal, such as a reindeer or an elk. The bones were attached to the boots with leather straps. This was unstable. To move

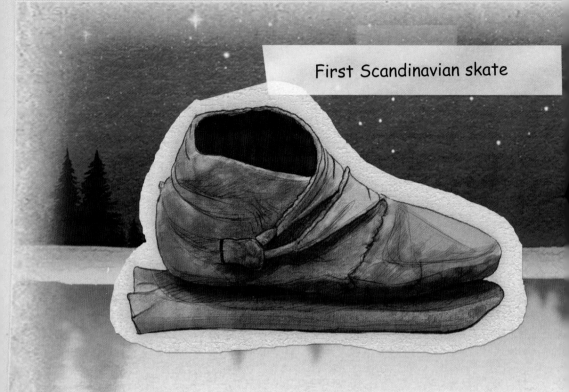

First Scandinavian skate

forward and stay balanced, the skater needed to use a stick!

The first skates with iron blades were also first made in Scandinavia, more than 1,700 years ago. A few hundred years later, the Vikings, who were a sailing people from the area, brought these skates to other parts of the world. Many countries improved upon them. Holland made the first skates with sharpened blades, in the 14th century.

Modern skate

From then on, skaters no longer needed a stick to help move them. A simple step was enough to send them gliding across the ice!

Now you know about the origins of ice skating. Keep practicing. You'll learn how to stop soon enough!

Your friend,
Professor Brainy

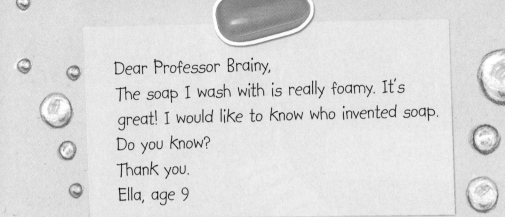

Dear Professor Brainy,
The soap I wash with is really foamy. It's great! I would like to know who invented soap. Do you know?
Thank you.
Ella, age 9

Dear Ella,

The story of soap goes back a long time. About 5,000 years ago, the Sumerians noticed that some oils, mixed with the ashes of plants, had the ability to clean. The mixture made a kind of soft soap. But this soap wasn't used for washing the body! People bathed with water, sand, and ashes that they then rinsed off. Soap was used for cleaning clothes and to treat skin problems, but not for bathing. The Gauls (ancient French) and the ancient Germans used soap for lightening their hair. It was only starting in the 2nd century that the Romans used soap to wash themselves.

Soap has changed a lot since then. The soap we wash with today is often made in factories. To get rid of dead skin and germs, we need to wash with soap regularly.

Today, there are all kinds of soaps and all types of scents to choose from. Some even contain olive oil or goat's milk.

Best wishes,
Professor Brainy

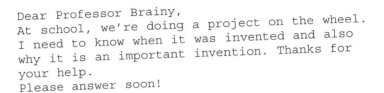

Subject: The wheel
To: Professor Brainy

Dear Professor Brainy,
At school, we're doing a project on the wheel.
I need to know when it was invented and also
why it is an important invention. Thanks for
your help.
Please answer soon!

Lea, age 12

Dear Lea,

My friend and I go on yearly
bicycle trips. We have visited
many beautiful places: Acadia
National Park in Maine, the
beaches of Hawaii, and
central Vermont.
You are probably
wondering why I
am telling you this!

Without the wheel, my friend and I could never have made all these trips. Why? Because no wheels means no bicycle! It's the same for all types of vehicles on wheels, like cars and buses. The wheel plays an important part in many other objects in our daily life. I can think of clocks, eggbeaters, and salad spinners, just to name a few.

Car

Bus

The wheel is considered one of the greatest human inventions. If you have other examples of objects that use a wheel, please send them to me! There must be hundreds of them.

Now, let's take a look at how the wheel was created.

Eggbeater

Circular saw

Watch

Salad spinner

The wheel was invented by the Sumerians 5,500 years ago. It first consisted of a slice of a tree trunk. It could also be made of wooden planks put together to form a circle. Over the centuries, the wheel became lighter and faster thanks to the invention of crossbars and then **spokes**.

Wheels looked different, depending on where and when they were used. I've drawn the first wheels for you here.

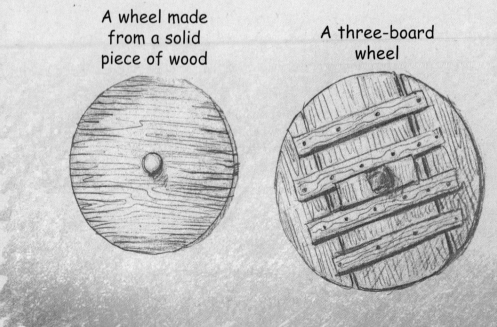

A wheel made from a solid piece of wood

A three-board wheel

Other paintings, as well as the remains of skis, were found in parts of Norway, northern Russia, and central Asia.

These clues tell us that skis were created in areas where winters were harsh and snowy. During this time, skiing was not a sport. It was a way to get around! Skis made it possible to move across the snow without sinking into it. For thousands of years, skiing was the only way for people of the northern countries to travel in the winter. Skis also allowed them to hunt and fish more easily. It was only in the 19th century that skiing became the fun pastime that we know today.

Best wishes,
Professor Brainy

Dear Professor Brainy,
Can you tell me what silk is?
Thanks,
Lucy, age 10

Hello, Lucy!

Silk is a soft and shiny thread that can be used to make fabric. According to an ancient legend, silk was discovered in China more than 4,600 years ago. The wife of the Chinese emperor Huangdi was seated in her garden under a mulberry tree. She was about to drink her tea when a cocoon fell into her cup. As she tried to remove it, she pulled a thread from the cocoon, which kept unraveling. She decided to weave the long thread. The resulting fabric was so soft and silky that she began raising the caterpillars that made these cocoons. That way, she could use their thread.

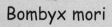

Bombyx mori

Amazing story, isn't it? Silk thread is produced by the **silkworm**, which is the caterpillar of a moth called Bombyx mori. Feeding off the leaves of the mulberry, the silkworm weaves a cocoon in order to become a moth. Silkworm farmers gather the cocoons and drop them into hot water to soften them. Then they brush the cocoons to make the silk thread unravel.

Silkworm

For thousands of years, the Chinese guarded the secret of silk making. Whoever revealed the secret to a stranger risked death. But in the year 555 two monks, returning to Europe after a trip to China, stole some silkworms.

Cocoon

They brought the silkworms back to Europe with them, and silk began to be made there as well. In spite of this, China remains one of the world's biggest silk producers.

Did you know, Lucy, that today we use silk made by other animals? The silk that spiders make, for example, is light and very strong. It is woven to make bulletproof vests.

Take care,
Professor Brainy

Dear Professor,
Who invented paper?
Alexander, age 9

Dear Alexander,

Let's take a trip back in time. Ever since people learned to draw and write, they've used all kinds of materials to express themselves. They started by carving and painting on rocks and bones. Then they traced symbols on wood, clay, and bamboo sticks.

The Egyptians were the first to use sheets made of **papyrus** stalks, more than 5,000 years ago! Papyrus is an a plant that grows on the banks of the Nile River. Light and strong, papyrus spread to other civilizations around the Mediterranean Sea.

— Papyrus

About 2,300 years ago, a new material called **parchment** was adopted in Pergamon, a city in Mysia (an ancient region of today's Turkey). Parchment is animal skin that has been stretched and dried. It was more expensive, but also stronger, than papyrus.

As for paper, it was invented in China about 2,100 years ago. You may have read in some books that it was invented around the year 105. However, ancient bits of paper that dated 200 years earlier were recently uncovered in the ruins of a village in northwestern China.

Parchment

The year 105 is still important because it was during this time that Cai Lun, a Chinese minister, wrote instructions to make paper. The art of papermaking remained a Chinese secret for more than 600 years. When the Arabs won the Battle of Talas in central Asia against the Chinese in 751, they took Chinese prisoners. Some of them were papermakers, who gave up the secret of papermaking to the victors.

So now you know all about it, my curious friend!

Yours truly,
Professor Brainy

Paper

Dear Professor Brainy,

My brother is in the third grade. He is learning multiplication tables. For him, the number 7 is hardest to multiply! Do you know who invented numbers?

Hope to hear from you soon!

Ivan, age 12

Dear Ivan,

When I was young, multiplication tables were hard for me, too. Tell your brother not to worry. Eventually these tables will sink in! But let's get back to your question.

About 6,000 years ago, the Sumerians used small clay objects for counting. Those objects are the oldest numerals we know of. Their shapes and sizes stood for different numbers. For example, a little cone represented the number 1. A bead was equal to 10. A big cone was equal to 60. Actually, Ivan, even the first human beings counted things—but in their own way. More than 20,000 years ago, humans were carving grooves into bones or rocks. They also marked off how many animals they had killed in the hunt. Long after the Sumerians, the Greeks, Romans, and Arabs were using a system with letters that stood for numbers. This numbering system appeared about 2,500 years ago. Here, for example, are several Roman numerals.

Roman Numerals and the Numbers They Represent

I = 1	VI = 6	L = 50
II = 2	VII = 7	C = 100
III = 3	VIII = 8	D = 500
IV = 4	IX = 9	M = 1,000
V = 5	X = 10	

Today, Roman numerals are usually used with the dates of movies and books, the names of boats (*Queen Mary II*), or the names of rulers and popes (Napoleon II or Pope Benedict XVI).

The earliest version of our 10 digits appeared in India about 2,200 years ago. They were called Brahmi numerals. People there invented a new symbol for each digit, one that was completely different from letters. Over time, these digits were refined. That is how we ended up with 0, 1, 2, 3, 4, 5, 6, 7, 8 and 9.

That's all for today. And give my best wishes to your brother!

Yours truly,
Professor Brainy

Dear Kim,

I think I recognize another chocolate fan! Did you know that chocolate is made from the fruit of a **cacao** tree? Cacao trees grow large, melon-sized fruit. They are shaped like footballs. About 25 seeds are in each fruit. Workers collect the seeds and let them dry. The hard, dried seeds are called cacao beans.

The dried cacao beans are sent to a factory. There they are cleaned and roasted. After, they are ground to form a soft liquid called cocoa butter. Chocolate bars are made from this butter.

Cacao pod

Cacao seeds

Cocoa beans

Ancient people called the Maya were the first people to use cacao beans. The Maya lived in the area that is now Mexico.

Cacao tree

The Maya made a drink by mixing the cacao beans with water and spices. It was called "xoxolatl" (pronounced "chocolate"). They drank it hot. It wasn't very sweet, but this drink was very popular. It could be flavored with other ingredients like honey, vanilla, or cinnamon.

Cacao beans were valuable to the Maya. They used the beans as money and gave them as gifts.

Chocolate crossed the Atlantic Ocean to Europe when Spanish explorer Hernán Cortés landed in the area in 1519. He did not like the taste at first, but once he added sugar to it, he found it delicious. He decided to bring it back to Europe.

Until next time, my young chocolate fan!

Professor Brainy

Dear Oliver,

Since ancient times, people have come up with clever ways for keeping things cold. More than 2,000 years ago, Alexander the Great, king of Macedonia (a country north of Greece) cooled barrels of wine in ditches filled with snow. Around the same time, the Greeks and Romans dug deep holes in the ground. They added ice and covered the holes with straw. That kept the ice from melting too quickly. Those early **icehouses** made it possible to chill food and preserve it for several months. Icehouses became more popular between the 17th and 19th centuries. To make an icehouse, a deep hole was dug in the ground. The walls were braced with stones and the structure was covered in a mound of earth. That provided better **insulation**. Take a look at the diagram of the icehouse I have drawn for you here.

How an Icehouse Worked

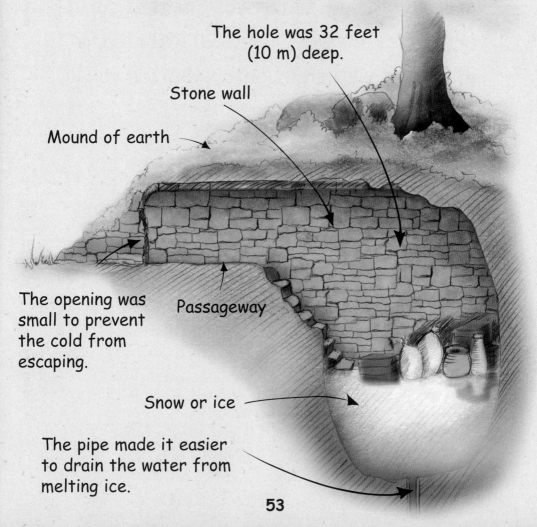

The hole was 32 feet (10 m) deep.

Stone wall

Mound of earth

The opening was small to prevent the cold from escaping.

Passageway

Snow or ice

The pipe made it easier to drain the water from melting ice.

Icehouses were used less and less once machines that made ice were invented in the 1850s. Food could then be kept cold inside the home. It was stored in wooden or steel cabinets containing blocks of ice. As for refrigerators, Oliver, the electric version we know today was created some years later. It was invented in the early 1920s by Swedish inventors Balzer von Platen and Carl Munters.

Best wishes,
Professor Brainy

Dear Professor Brainy,
What were the first jobs? When did people
start doing them?
Thank you!

Audrey, age 12

Dear Audrey,

It seems that the first job, or trade, appeared in the Fertile Crescent. This is a region in the Middle East. Twelve thousand years ago, the climate in this part of the world became milder and more humid. Land that had been dry, cold desert could now grow crops. Grains, like wheat and barley, began filling entire fields. This was a big change from the deserts that people from that region knew. Before, they had to be on the move all the time, searching

for food. Now, with all this food around, there was no longer any need to go in search of it!

The people of the Fertile Crescent decided to settle in a more permanent way. This is how the first villages came to be built, about 11,000 years ago. Over time, the populations of the villages grew. Soon, there was not enough food to feed everyone just by hunting and gathering grains. People had the idea to gather seeds from these grains and to replant them. In this way, about 10,000 years ago, people started growing grain and raising livestock. They were the first farmers!

Other kinds of activities became a normal part of village life. Some villagers made bricks and built houses. Others made pottery to hold food, or became bakers. These were the first trades!

By the way, Audrey, what kind of job would you like to have someday?

Your friend,
Professor Brainy

Dear Professor Brainy,

My parents and I are moving to a bigger house because I am going to have a new little brother. I can't wait! Can you please tell me who invented houses?

Thank you.

Brett, age 10

Dear Brett,

My very best wishes to you and your family! Before houses appeared, people lived in caves or huts. Huts were made out of bones or branches and covered with animal skins. Eleven thousand years ago, when people were settling in permanent villages, they left their temporary huts. They built dwellings that were more solid and long-lasting. Those early houses were built with bricks of clay and straw that had been molded and dried in the sun. About 3,000 years later, the Sumerians built houses that were more advanced. They were also more sturdy. The bricks they used were baked in an oven. Sumerians assembled the bricks using a natural tar that worked like cement.

Over time, houses changed. Second floors appeared, as did heating, and bathrooms were added. Little by little, houses were given all the modern comforts you know today.

All the best, Brett, and be sure to take good care of your little brother!

Professor Brainy

Dear Professor Brainy,
When were the first toys
invented?
Thank you,
Zoë, age 11

Dear Zoë,

I have always been amazed by
the wide variety of toys that are
found around the world. The oldest
toys we know of were dug up by
archaeologists in Egypt. They are
about 4,500 years old. Actually,
Zoë, even if we haven't found
traces of toys that are older,
it doesn't mean that none
existed before.

Egyptian children enjoyed playing with hoops, dolls, dice, and small animals on wheels. Chinese children liked to play with kites. Kites have been found in China that are 3,500 years old. As many as 2,500 years ago, Greek children had fun with yo-yos, tops, and swings. Roman children played with dolls, rattles, toy dishes, and other items for "playing house."

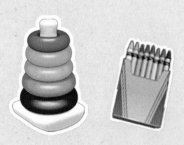

As you must have noticed, many of these games still exist today! They have been amusing children for thousands of years. Quite impressive, isn't it? And how about you, Zoë? What are your favorite toys?

Your friend,
Professor Brainy

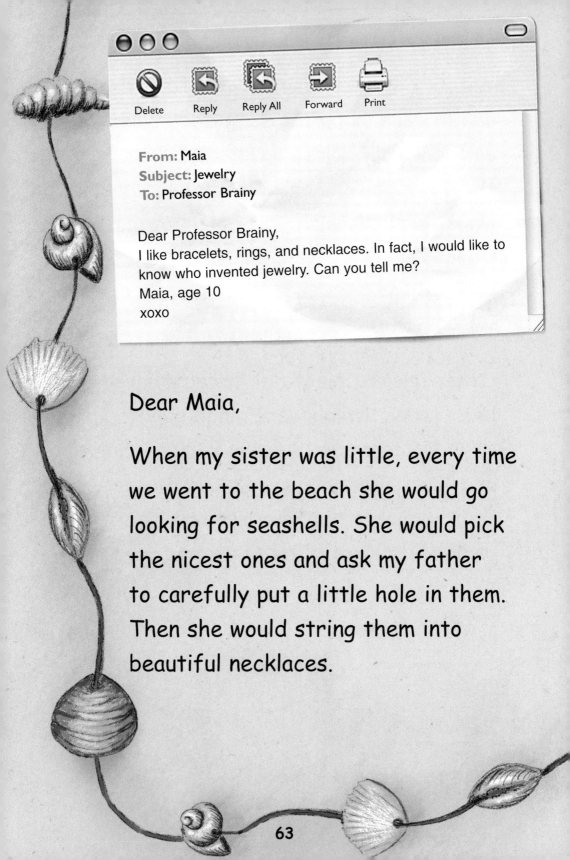

From: Maia
Subject: Jewelry
To: Professor Brainy

Dear Professor Brainy,
I like bracelets, rings, and necklaces. In fact, I would like to know who invented jewelry. Can you tell me?
Maia, age 10
xoxo

Dear Maia,

When my sister was little, every time we went to the beach she would go looking for seashells. She would pick the nicest ones and ask my father to carefully put a little hole in them. Then she would string them into beautiful necklaces.

Without even realizing it, my father and sister were using the same techniques as the world's first jewelers! In fact, the oldest pieces of jewelry discovered were seashells with holes pierced in them. They were found in 2002 in a cave in South Africa. Those shells are more than 75,000 years old!

Other ancient pieces of jewelry have been found, which were made about 35,000 years ago by early humans. Some of these pieces were skillfully crafted. It is thought that jewelry from this period was related to a person's age,

social status, or the tribe to which he or she belonged. Today's jewelry is mainly worn for decoration.

So there's your answer, Maia!

All the best,
Professor Brainy

Dear Professor Brainy,

Do you know who invented heating in houses?

Thank you.
Bernard, age 12

Dear Bernard,

When humans discovered fire, they quickly realized that it gave off heat. People have since used fire to warm themselves and their homes. In ancient times small fires were used to heat the insides of huts and early homes. One of the most important inventions

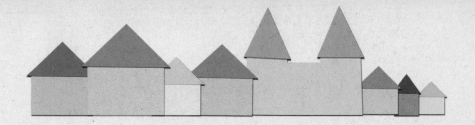

for heating homes was the **hypocaust**. The hypocaust was the earliest form of central heating. This kind of heating can warm an entire house from a single source. The heat is sent to different rooms through a series of pipes.

The hypocaust was created in ancient Greece about 2,500 years ago. Around the year 100, however, it was perfected by the Romans. The hypocaust heats a house at floor level. I have drawn a diagram on the two pages that follow.

Until next time,
Professor Brainy

How A Hypocaust Worked

The walls were made of hollow bricks. The warm air continued on its course through hollow walls and was then released to the outdoors through a kind of chimney.

A fire outside the house heated the air.

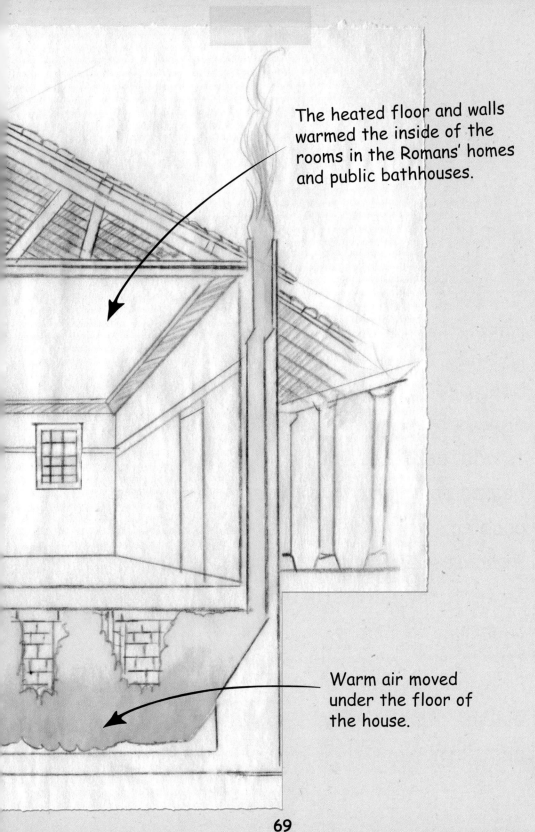

The heated floor and walls warmed the inside of the rooms in the Romans' homes and public bathhouses.

Warm air moved under the floor of the house.

Dear Amelia,

Your dad is right! The Chinese invented the **abacus** 5,000 years ago. This tool was used to add, subtract, multiply, and divide. It even helped solve some of the same tough math problems that today's calculators solve. Abacuses work just as well as calculators. In fact, they are still used today in some countries in Asia.

Do you know what kind of abacus your father bought, Amelia? There are several kinds. The best known are the Chinese abacus (suanpan),

Chinese abacus

the Japanese abacus (soroban), and the Russian abacus (schoty). The Chinese and Japanese abacuses have a wooden frame. Inside the frame are several rods on which beads can slide. The beads are divided into two sections by a central bar.

Let's take a look at how to read a number on one of these abacuses. (You can follow along by looking at my illustration on the next page.) Each rod represents the position of a digit in the number. It starts from the right with the single digits, then the tens, hundreds, thousands, etc.

Next, each bead located under the central bar has the value of 1. Those that are above the bar are worth 5. The idea is to count only the beads that are lying against the central bar. I have drawn an example with a Chinese abacus representing the number 7,925.

Your friend,
Professor Brainy

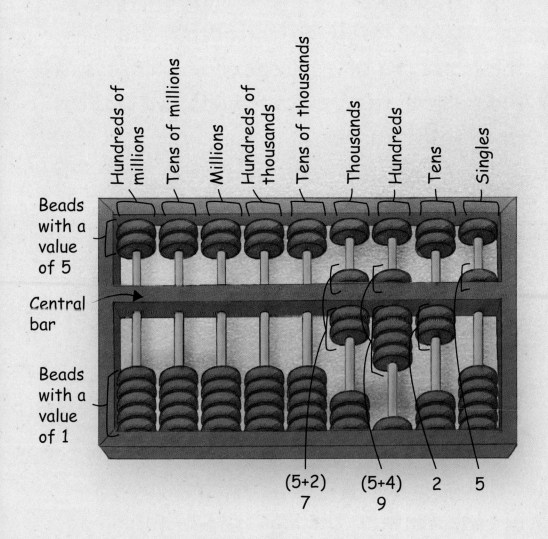

Dear Professor Brainy,
Did prehistoric people brush their teeth with toothpaste?
Thank you.
Jonathan, age 10

Dear Jonathan,

I hope you won't be disappointed, but prehistoric humans did not know about toothpaste! Many people in ancient times were concerned about the health of their teeth, however. The earliest clue that toothpaste existed is on a sheet of Egyptian papyrus that is about 3,500 years old. It is one of the oldest medical texts ever found. Besides describing different illnesses, this papyrus had many recipes for toothpaste. Ingredients included dirt and honey.

Egyptians rubbed the mixture on their teeth with their fingers or with a little stick.

Other countries had their own toothpaste recipes, too. In Greece, chalk was used to whiten teeth. A toothpaste made of a mixture of pepper and lentils was also recommended. Roman doctors prescribed various mixtures of powdered deer antler, coal, seashells, and pumice stone.

Today we've discovered many modern toothpaste formulas. They are very different from those of ancient times! One of the biggest changes made in toothpaste is that it not only cleans, but also helps prevent cavities. That's something the old toothpaste formulas never did!

And so, there's your answer, my friend. Don't forget to brush twice a day. Flossing your teeth once a day also keeps them healthy!

Best wishes,
Professor Brainy

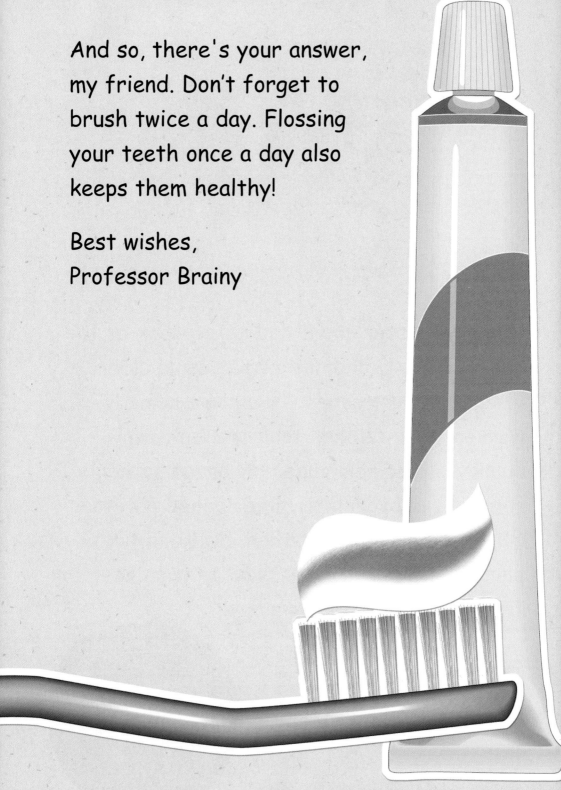

Dear Professor Brainy,
I would like to know how people
cured illnesses before medicine was
invented.
Thanks, Professor!
Laurie, age 12

Dear Laurie,

When my sister and I had chickenpox at the
age of 6, my grandmother put apple cider
vinegar on our rashes. This home remedy
worked very well and took the itch away
quickly. I also remember my grandmother's
remedy for bronchitis. She cooked potatoes,
mashed them, and put them between two
cloths. She put this dressing on the chest for
two hours, three times a day!

My grandmother's remedies
were passed down to her by
her grandmothers and her
great-grandmothers. She
really believed in these natural
medicines.

I'm telling you these stories
because they are an example
of how people used to turn to
nature to treat what ailed them.

Witch-hazel
leaves

More than 6,000 years ago, the Sumerians used
the leaves of the white willow tree to treat
pain. Native Americans used witch-hazel to stop
bleeding and to soothe burns. Before modern
medicine, people treated themselves with these
and many other natural remedies.

As a matter of fact, Laurie, the chemists who made the first medicines were mainly inspired by old remedies. Aspirin, for example, was made from the leaves of the white willow. In a way, the Sumerians discovered aspirin before the rest of the world did!

Take care,
Professor Brainy

White willow leaves

Dear Professor Brainy,
I really like mailing you letters! I have a question: Has mail been around for a long time? What about e-mail?
I'll be waiting for your reply.
Thanks!
Sam, age 11

Dear Sam,

I really like getting letters from curious young readers like you!

The history of the mail goes back a long time. The Egyptians were sending messengers across their country 4,000 years ago. They carried messages from one city to the next. Other people in ancient times, like the Chinese, the Persians, and the Greeks, organized the same kind of postal service.

The Romans had a highly developed postal system a little more than 2,000 years ago. At the time, Sam, there were not as many roads as there are today. Messengers traveled on horseback. The mail could take several days to reach its destination. To improve the service, the Romans built relay stations along the routes. These stations were inns where the messengers could rest, eat, and get fresh horses. This system was kept in place until the invention of the railroad at the beginning of the 19th century.

Ever since, mail has been traveling more quickly. It is sorted at night and delivered the next day. Today, you can send messages by mail, but you can also use the Internet. That way, messages are delivered even faster! I still have a soft spot for the postal service, though. It gives me a chance to see what your nice handwriting looks like!

Best regards,
Professor Brainy

Dear Toshi,

We don't know exactly when or how music was invented. The first musical instruments were the hands and the feet. Clues from the past tell us that nature inspired early humans. Simple objects like seashells, pieces of bone, or wood could be used to make sounds. Archaeologists have uncovered a large number of bones with holes in them. These were used as flutes.

Paintings on walls in some caves in Europe show that music was part of prehistoric life. Take a look at this pamphlet from the Museum of Natural History. This painting was made more than 15,000 years ago in a cave in southern France.

Trois Frères cave, Ariège, France

Behind the animals running away, there is a figure disguised as a bison, playing a bow harp (an ancestor of the harp we know today).

In spite of all these clues, no one really knows what purpose music served to prehistoric people. Was it used to imitate birdcalls for hunting? Did it mark certain rituals or practices? Did it honor important moments in life, such as birth and death? I imagine that it was a mother who invented the lullaby one night when her baby was crying more than usual.

Yours truly,
Professor Brainy

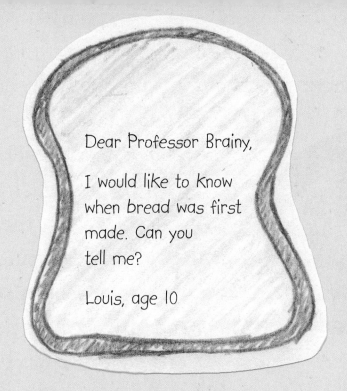

Dear Professor Brainy,

I would like to know when bread was first made. Can you tell me?

Louis, age 10

Hello, Louis!

I would like to answer your question, but even scientists who study ancient cultures don't know when bread was first made. The oldest bread oven that we know of was built almost 8,000 years ago. It was found in an ancient city in Turkey. The bread baked there was a **flatbread** made of cereal flour. The kind of bread we eat today, with a crust and a soft center, was made 5,000 years ago by the Egyptians.

I remember reading a legend about bread many years ago. Here is the story: One evening, an Egyptian baker left some gruel (wet cereal) out in the open. Over a few hours, a microscopic organism spoiled the mixture. The next day, the baker noticed that the mixture had doubled in size. He baked it anyway! Taking it out of the oven, he tasted the bread and liked its lightness and flavor. And that's how bread was first created.

You may be asking yourself
why the mixture swelled
up. It's quite simple!
Bread is made with flour,
water, salt, and **yeast**.
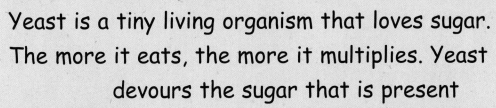
Yeast is a tiny living organism that loves sugar.
The more it eats, the more it multiplies. Yeast
devours the sugar that is present
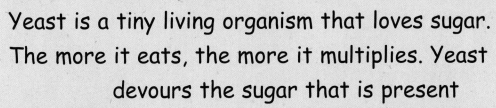
in the flour. While doing this,
the yeast gives off gas. It
is this gas that makes the
dough rise and that forms
tiny bubbles in the soft part
of the bread. This process is
called **fermentation**.

Other countries learned about this new bread, and soon couldn't live without it! Ever since, people have continued to invent bread recipes and baking techniques. Today, there are almost as many varieties of bread as there are countries!

Best wishes,
Professor Brainy

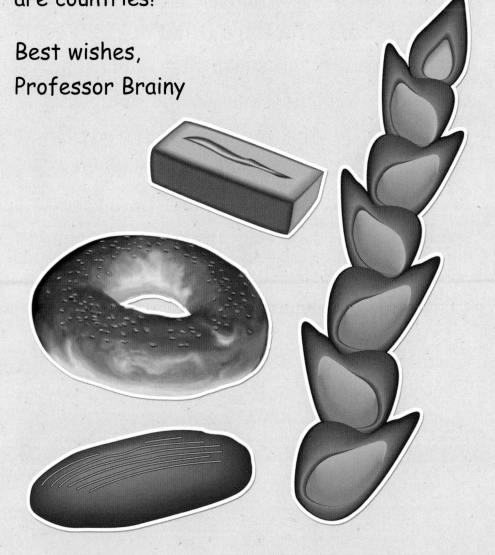

Dear Professor Brainy,
How long have knives, forks, and spoons been around?
Thank you.
Luca, age 9

Dear Luca,

When I was a kid, I was always asking my parents if I could eat my dinner with my fingers. But prehistoric humans ate with their fingers every day!

Knives, forks, and spoons have been around a very long time. What's funny, Luca, is that these utensils were not invented for using at the table. They were intended for cooking, serving meals, and in the case of the knife—self-defense!

The earliest knives were invented in prehistoric times. People needed to cut and slice the meat they brought back from the hunt. By carving a stone very finely, they got a tool that was extremely sharp. Metal knives made their appearance more than 7,000 years ago. The first table knife goes back to about the year 1,000. Back then, it was something only wealthy people used.

As for the spoon, scientists believe it is about 20,000 years old. At this time, people ate a lot of gruel, which was similar to oatmeal. You can imagine that eating gruel with their hands was pretty messy! People used seashells and the hard shells of fruit as spoons. Slowly, people began making spoons out of wood, bone, and metal.

The first forks appeared in ancient times. The Egyptians and Romans used a hook to spear meat cooking in large pots. The Romans, along with the Greeks, used a large, two-tined fork to hold the meat while it was being cut.

It was only at the end of the 17th century that the fork was regularly used as an eating utensil. Over time, the fork became smaller and gained more tines. The fork remained a luxury item until the 18th century.

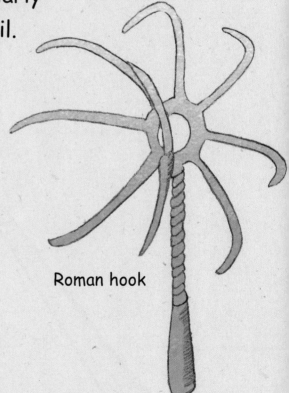

Roman hook

And so, Luca, there you have the history of the knife, fork, and spoon. I'll be waiting for more questions from you!

All the best,
Professor Brainy

Dear Jennifer,

I have always said that a summer without ice cream just wouldn't feel like summer!

Ice cream appeared in China more than 5,000 years ago. It was a mixture of fruit, honey, and snow. It seems, Jennifer, that ancient people had as much of a "sweet tooth" as we do! More than 2,000 years ago, the kings of Baghdad ate fruit syrup chilled with snow. The Arabs called these chilled syrups "sharbets." This is where we get the word sherbet. In Macedonia, King Alexander the Great served his guests diced fruit mixed with honey and snow. I also like the story of Emperor Nero, who ruled Rome 2,000 years ago. He loved snow flavored with fruit juice and honey. Before every party, Nero sent workers to the top of the Apennine Mountains to bring back snow. These mountains were located some 248 miles (400 km) from Rome! Quite a long way to go for dessert, wasn't it?

It is said that the Italian explorer Marco Polo returned from his trip to China with the recipe for the ice cream we know today. It was intended for Italian kings, but ice cream was a huge hit among the rest of the population.

Ice cream's popularity spread through Europe and later to America.

And so, Jennifer, now you know everything about how ice cream was invented! By the way, my favorite flavor is chocolate.

Best wishes,
Professor Brainy

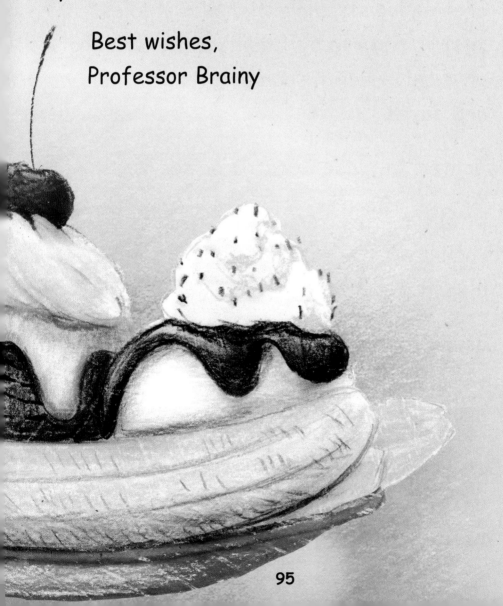

Glossary

abacus a device for making arithmetic calculations, consisting of a set of rods on which beads are moved

archaeologist a scientist who studies past human life by finding and examining physical remains, such as pottery, tools, and bones

barter to trade in goods or services

biface a stone tool, often made of flint rock, with two faces, or sides, that form a point

cacao a tropical tree that produces seeds, also called cocoa beans, used to make chocolate

chopper a stone carved with the help of another stone to make it sharp

⌒ Glossary ⌒

cuneiform a wedge-shaped style of writing developed by the Sumerians

discovery something that is seen or understood for the first time, but that already existed in nature

fermentation the process by which yeast converts sugar into carbon dioxide and alcohol

flatbread a kind of bread made without yeast and baked in flat loaves

hypocaust a home heating system in which warm air is circulated through hollow spaces in the floor or walls

icehouse a structure for storing ice, typically used to preserve food

Glossary

incense material used to produce a perfume when burned

insulation the surrounding of a space or body with material designed to prevent the entrance or escape of energy

invention something created by a person that did not exist before, such as a tool

papyrus an aquatic plant that grows on the banks of the Nile River used by Egyptians to make a kind of paper

parchment animal skin that has been stretched and dried to form a material on which to write

Phoenicians an ancient people who developed a culture on the east coast of the Mediterranean Sea 3,300 years ago

Glossary

silk a thread made from the cocoon of the silkworm and used to make fabric

silkworm the caterpillar of a moth called "Bombyx mori," which feeds off the leaves of the mulberry tree and whose cocoon is used to produce silk

spokes the rods that connect the hub of a wheel to its rim

Sumerians an ancient civilization that thrived on the banks of the Tigris and Euphrates rivers in what is now Iraq

yeast a tiny living organism that eats sugar and converts it into carbon dioxide and alcohol, causing dough to rise

For More Information

Books:

1,000 Inventions & Discoveries. Roger Bridgman (DK Publishing, New York, 2006)

Ancient Egypt (Nature Company Discoveries Libraries). George Hart (editor) (Time-Life Books, 1995)

Amazing Leonardo da Vinci Inventions You Can Build Yourself (Build It Yourself). Maxine Anderson (Nomad Press, 2006)

Cool Stuff and How It Works. Chris Woodford, Ben Morgan, and Clint Witchalls (DK Publishing, New York, 2005)

Invention (DK Eyewitness Books). Lionel Bender, (DK Publishing, New York, 2005)

For More Information

Web sites:

BBC Ancient History

www.bbc.co.uk/history/ancient

How Stuff Works

www.howstuffworks.com

Smith College's Museum of Ancient Inventions

www.smith.edu/hsc/museum/ancient_
inventions/hsclist.htm

ThinkQuest's Ancient Chinese Technology

library.thinkquest.org/23062/index.html

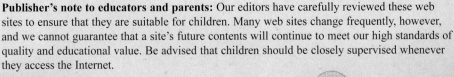

Index

Index